GW01269761

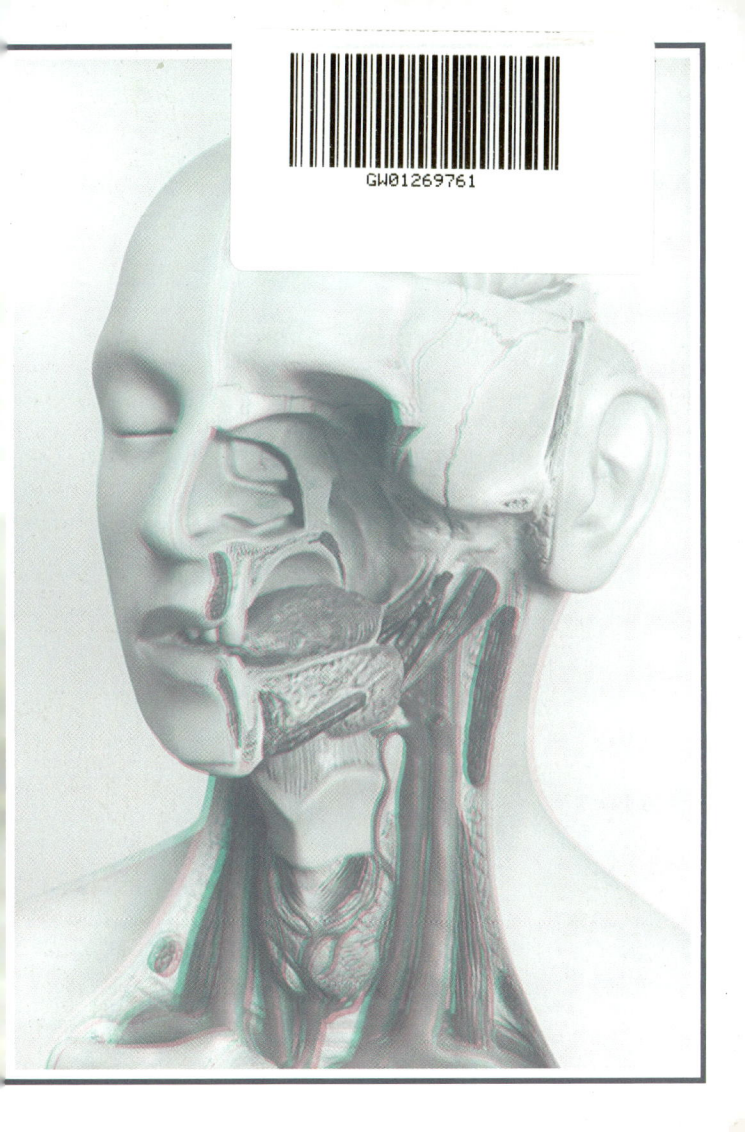

SKELETON

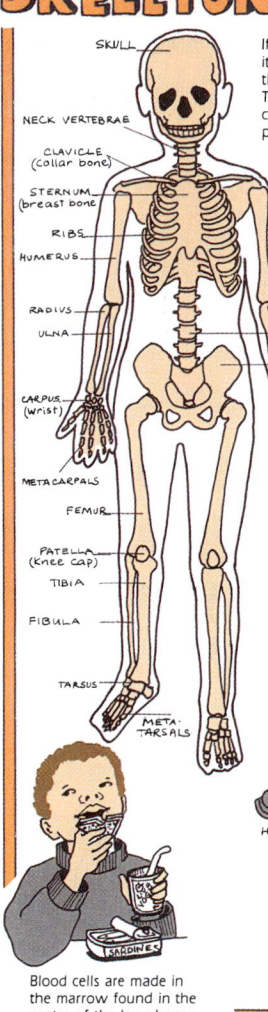

Skeleton labels (front view):
- SKULL
- NECK VERTEBRAE
- CLAVICLE (collar bone)
- STERNUM (breast bone)
- RIBS
- HUMERUS
- RADIUS
- ULNA
- LUMBAR VERTEBRAE
- PELVIS (hip)
- CARPUS (wrist)
- METACARPALS
- FEMUR
- PATELLA (knee cap)
- TIBIA
- FIBULA
- TARSUS
- METATARSALS

If you remove the poles from a tent, it would collapse. The poles support the thin canvas and give it shape. The bones which make up our frame, called the skeleton, support the softer parts of our body like the poles of a tent.

Our bones also protect the softer parts of the body from getting squashed or bumped. Our ribs protect our heart and lungs; the skull protects our brain and our backbone protects our nerve cord.

Spine labels:
- CERVICAL VERTEBRAE — Allow head and neck movement
- THORACIC VERTEBRAE — Support rib cage. Allow bending and rotation of trunk
- LUMBAR VERTEBRAE — Allow bending and rotation of trunk
- SACRAL VERTEBRAE — Fused together, distribute weight of body to hips and legs
- COCCYX

Arm labels (bent arm with muscles):
- BICEPS
- SCAPULA shoulder blade
- HUMERUS
- RADIUS
- TRICEPS
- ULNA

Our bones provide places for muscles to be attached. Muscles contract and pull against the bones causing movement at the joints. This allows you to move your whole body, or parts of it, when you want to.

Calcium-rich foods help keep bones strong and healthy.

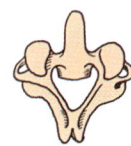

VERTEBRA WHERE THE NERVE CORD RUNS THROUGH

Joint types:
- HINGE
- PIVOT
- BALL AND SOCKET
- SLIDE

A normal adult has 206 bones and every bone (except one) is connected to another in its own special way. Some do not move; others move like hinges, pivots or balls in sockets.

Blood cells are made in the marrow found in the centre of the long bones.

Put on your glasses now and see a skeleton on opposite page.

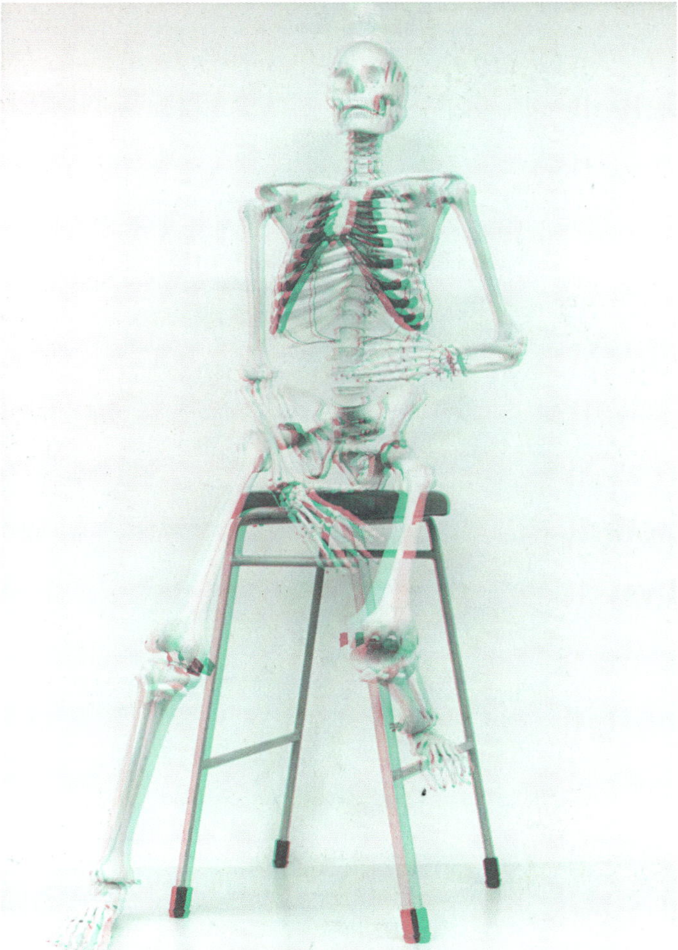

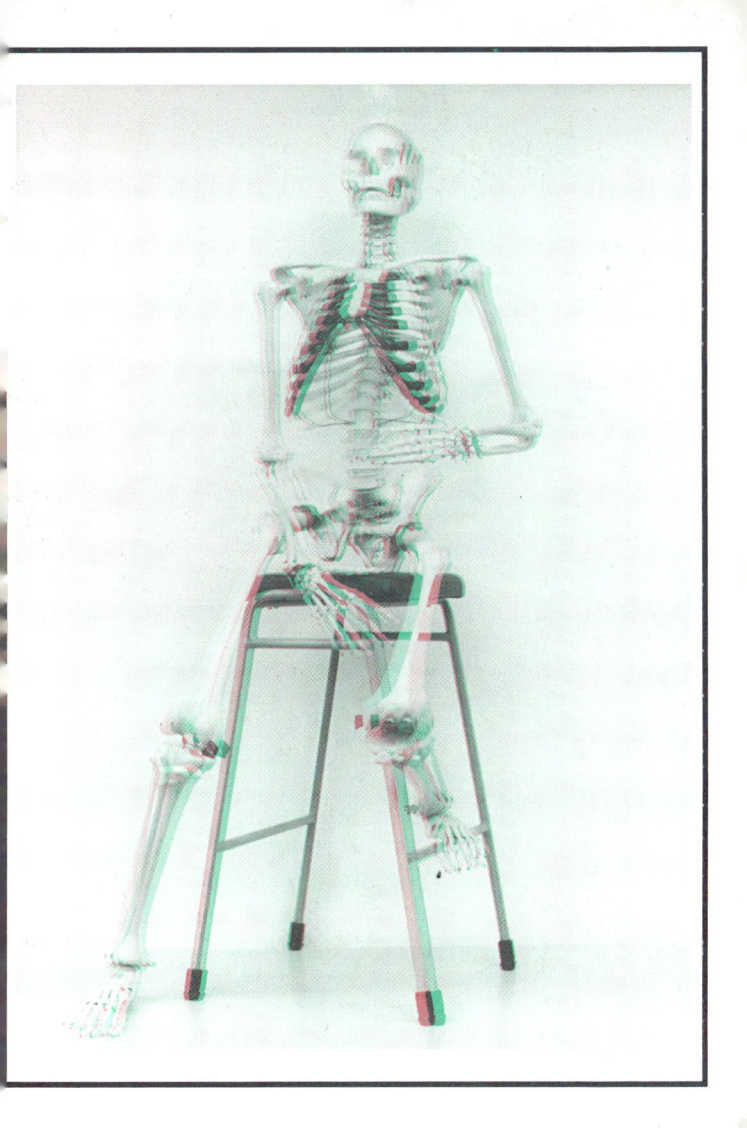

BLOOD

The blood in your body doesn't just wash around in there but travels through every bit of your body inside tubes called arteries and veins. You can see these on the inside of your wrist.

Blood takes food and oxygen to every corner of your body. It collects used oxygen (carbon dioxide) and waste food, and takes them away.

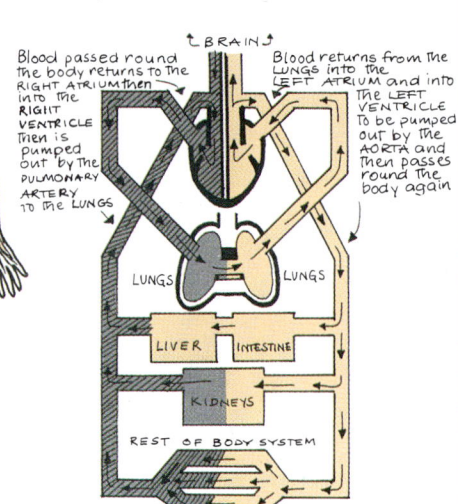

LUNGS
HEART

BRAIN

Blood passed round the body returns to the RIGHT ATRIUM then into the RIGHT VENTRICLE then is pumped out by the PULMONARY ARTERY to the LUNGS

Blood returns from the LUNGS into the LEFT ATRIUM and into the LEFT VENTRICLE to be pumped out by the AORTA and then passes round the body again

LUNGS LUNGS
LIVER INTESTINE
KIDNEYS
REST OF BODY SYSTEM

Blood is like a lot of trains carrying things around in tunnels inside you.

Your heart is the pump which pushes the blood along each time it beats.

RIGHT ATRIUM
AORTA
PULMONARY ARTERY
LEFT ATRIUM
RIGHT VENTRICLE
LEFT VENTRICLE

Your heart is divded into four chambers, like rooms. The top chambers, called atria, receive blood either from the lungs or the body: the bottom chambers, called the ventricles, pump blood out of the heart and all around the body.

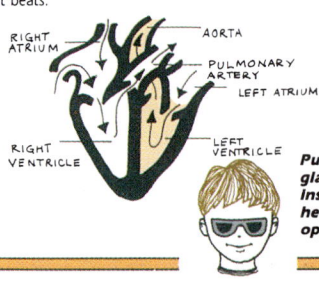

Put on your glasses to see the inside of your heart on the opposite page.

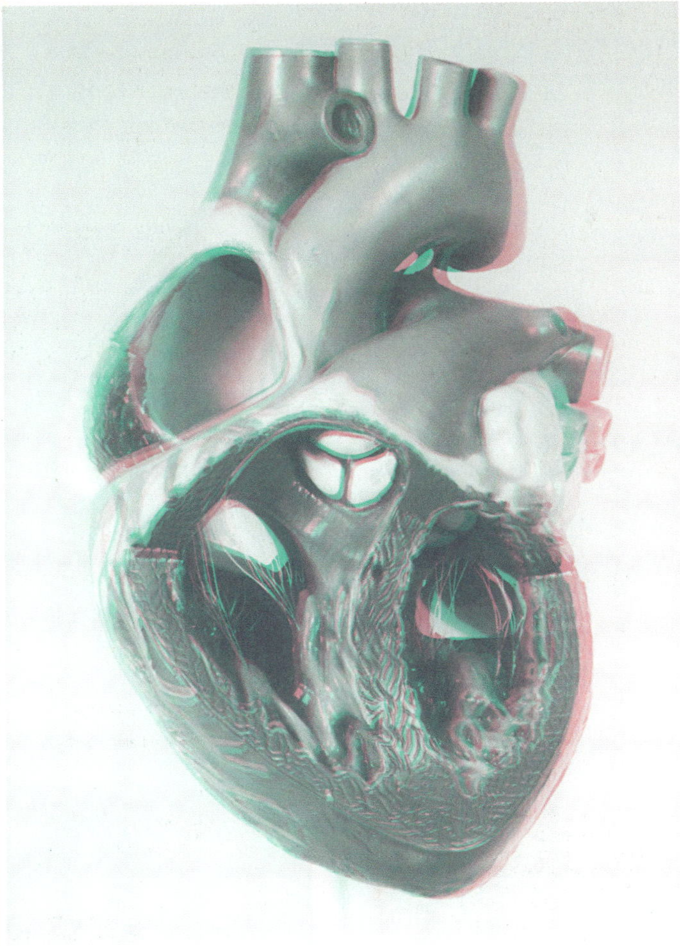

LUNGS

We breathe air to keep us alive. In the air, there are different kinds of invisible gas. We need fresh supplies of one of these gases, oxygen, all the time.

We get oxygen into our body by breathing it through our nose or mouth. Air then passes into our windpipe or trachea which divides into two branches called the right and left bronchi. One bronchus goes to each lung. We have two of these squashy, spongy bags in our chest.

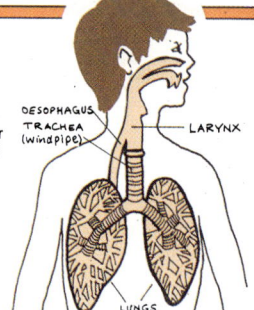

When you breathe out, called expiration, the ribs go down to push the air out.

Exercise makes you breathe hard because it uses up more oxygen than sitting down, so you pant to catch more air.

Every time you breathe in, called inspiration, your ribs go up and out making your chest bigger. Air is pulled in through your nose or mouth to fill up the bigger space.

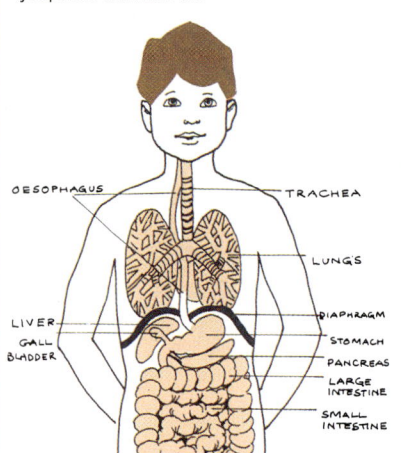

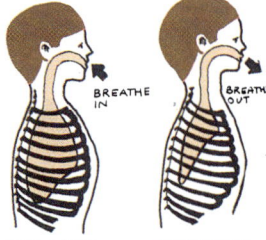

INSPIRATION   EXPIRATION

Put on your glasses to see the inside of your chest on the opposite page.

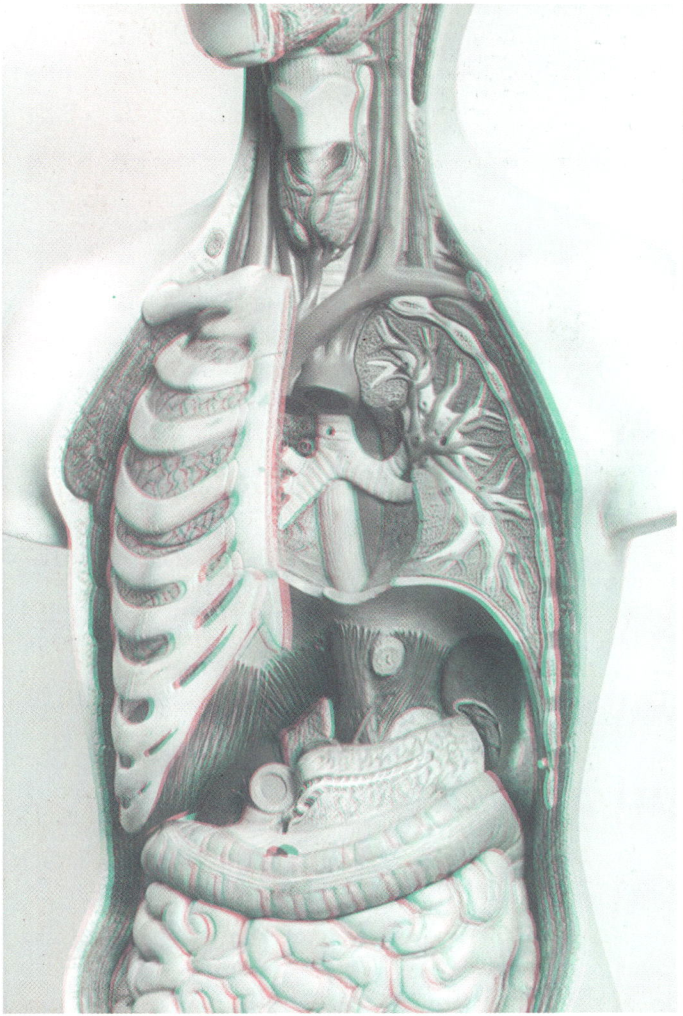

EARS

Your ear not only picks up sound waves, but also holds liquid which helps control your balance.

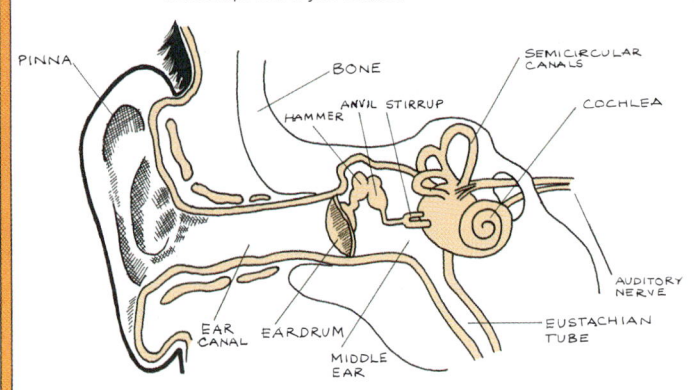

Labels on diagram: PINNA, BONE, HAMMER, ANVIL, STIRRUP, SEMICIRCULAR CANALS, COCHLEA, AUDITORY NERVE, EUSTACHIAN TUBE, MIDDLE EAR, EARDRUM, EAR CANAL

Sound waves make the air in the outer ear and the eardrum vibrate. The vibration then passes into the cochlea (your inner ear) which is sensitive to sound waves. Cells there send messages along a nerve to the brain which decodes the sounds.

Your balance is steady when you move normally, as the liquid in your ear stays level.

When your head moves suddenly, the liquid sloshes about. This sends a message to your brain telling it what is happening, but which can be confused, as when you spin round and round.

When you stop the liquid continues to spin making you think you are still moving.

***Turn book on its side.
Put on your glasses to view
your ear on the opposite page.***

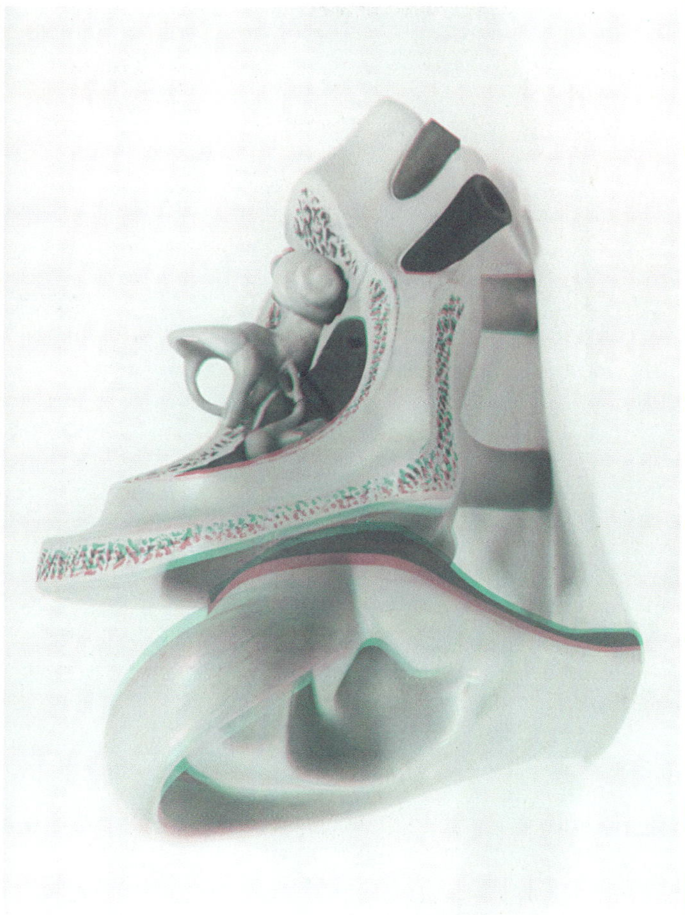

EYES

Your eyes work rather like a camera. There is a lens in front, and a coating at the back very like a film. This is called the retina and is 'wired up' to your brain so that your mind can see what is sensed by your eyes.

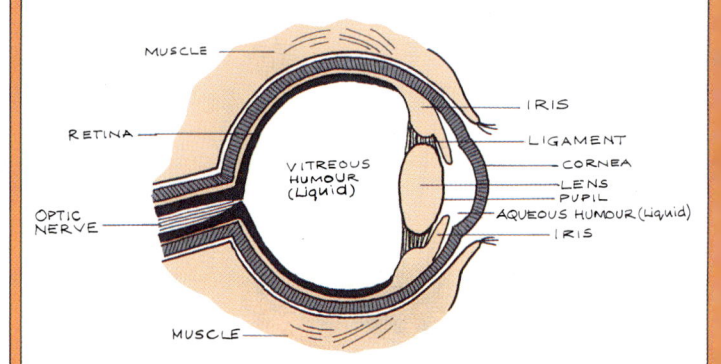

Diagram labels: MUSCLE, RETINA, OPTIC NERVE, VITREOUS HUMOUR (Liquid), MUSCLE, IRIS, LIGAMENT, CORNEA, LENS, PUPIL, AQUEOUS HUMOUR (Liquid), IRIS

The rest of the eye protects the retina, or focuses light on it.
   The lens of your eye works automatically, to focus on near or far things. It is inside your pupil, the little black hole in the middle of the coloured part (the iris). Each eye is set in a bony socket in the skull, called the orbit.

Just like the aperture in a camera the size of the pupil changes to suit bright or dim light.

Turn book on its side.
Put on your glasses to see the back
of an eye on the opposite page.

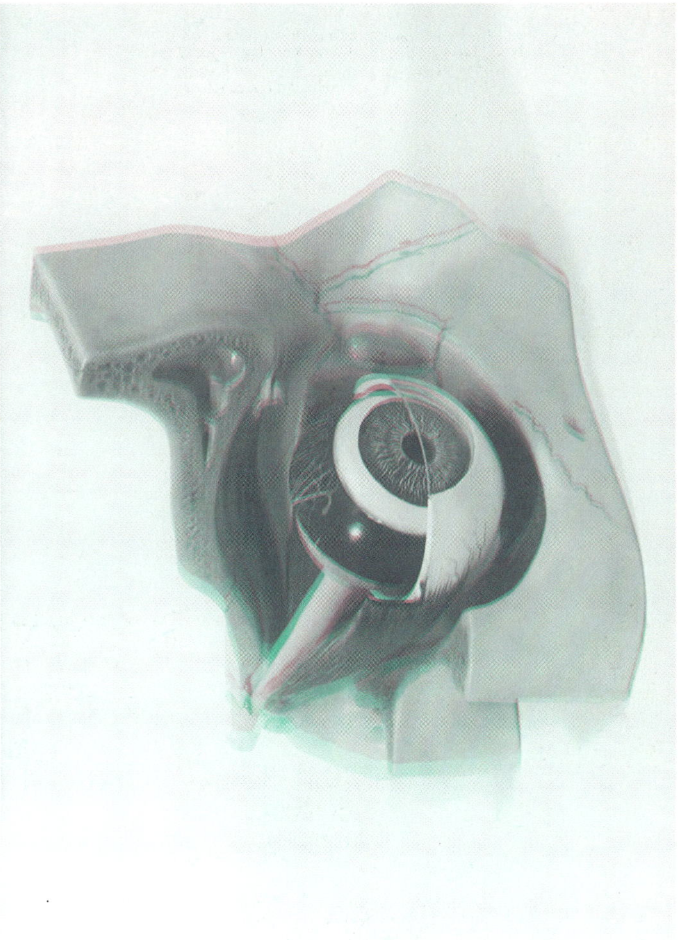

| AA | BB | CC | DD | EE | FF | GG | HH | II | JJ | KK | LL |

| 1 | 2 | 3 | 4 | 5 | 6 | 7 | 8 | 9 | 10 | 11 | 12 |

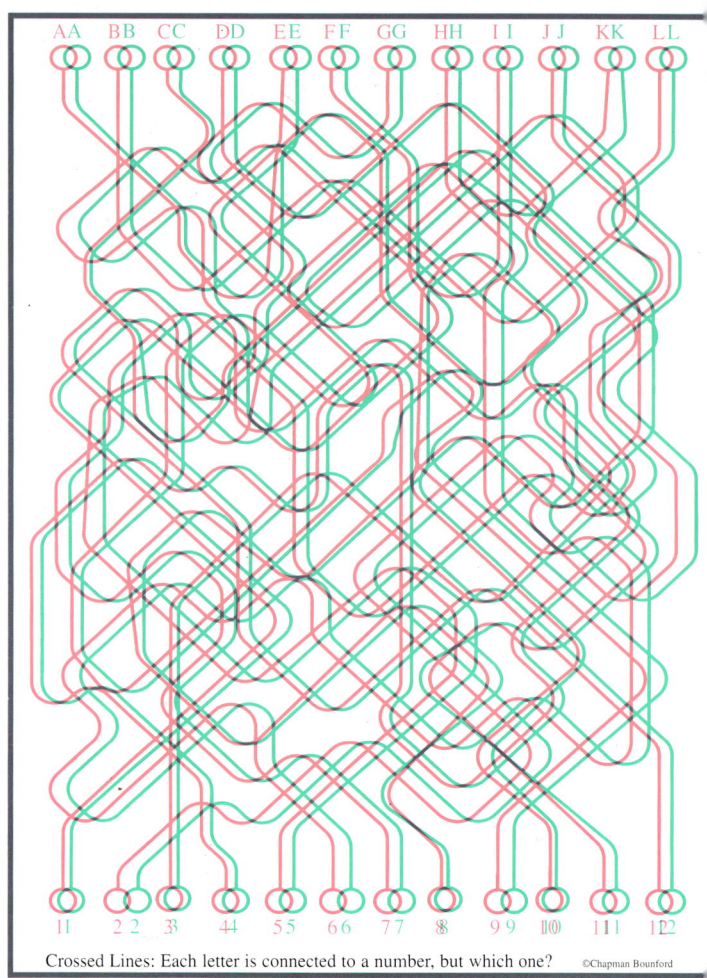

Crossed Lines: Each letter is connected to a number, but which one? ©Chapman Bounford

First Published by ©Claiborne Publications U.K.Ltd. in 1993
Written by Michele Claiborne. Illustrated by Shirley McLaughlin. 3D Photography by David Burder.
This Edition Published by Tobar Limited ©1999